The Diffusion Process

Process

DEVOTIONAL JOURNAL

RUBY TRAITS INCLUDED

AMAZING RARE RUBIES

About The Author

Meca McLendon, CLC is a certified life coach, financial mentor, radio host and Founder & CEO of Amazing Rare Rubies, LLC.

As a result of an amazing encounter with God, and her passion for helping women to become the woman God created them to be.

Amazing Rare Rubies,LLC was conceived in 2000, birthed in 2014 and officially launched in 2015. Meca has over 25 years of experience in lead-

About The Author

ership coaching, training and personal & professional development. She is well-known in her community for her talents and has been a featured guest with various radio and TV media outlets such as 108 Praise Radio, WYZE Radio, Bizlynks TV and more. She has hosted two radio shows: *The After Care Show* on WDRB Media & *A Ruby In The Making Show* on All Nations Radio.

Meca resides in Atlanta, Georgia with her husband, Lautrice McLendon, three children: Jerica, Blair & Jericia and two grandchildren: London & Landon

Today, Meca strives to be a living example of an Amazing Rare Ruby, a woman who fears the Lord and who is always becoming........

The Diffusion Process Devotional Journal 1st Edition December 2018 Copyright© 2018 Amazing Rare Rubies

All rights reserved. No part of this book may be reproduced, stored in a retrevial system or transmitted in any form or by any means (including electronic, mechanical, photocopying, recording, or otherwise) without prior written permission from the publisher.

Cover & Page Design by Noah Rae Graphics
Editing & Publishing by Nancy Publisher

ISBN: 9781792039980

To all of the Rubies in the making,

This devotional journal is dedicated to you. I want you to know that you are fearfully and wonderfully made and everything you need to become is inside of you waiting to be cultivated. It is time for you to start your journey to becoming the woman you were created to be and I am so honored that we are going to journey together, as we are Rubies in the making.

With Ruby Love,

Meca

Ruby Traits

Beautiful	1
Comfort	5
Courage	9
Creative	13
Decision Making	17
Determination	21
Diligent	25
Ethical	29
Faith	33
Focus	37
Forgiveness	41
Giving	45
Humble	49
Loving	53
Obedience	57
Patience	61
Prepared	65
Selfless	69
Thrifty	73
Stable Minded	77
Strong	81
Thoughtful	85
Timely	89
Trustworthy	93
Wisdom	97

Introduction

"Consider it nothing but joy, my brothers and sisters, whenever you fall into various trials. Be assured that the testing of your faith [through experience] produces endurance [leading to spiritual maturity, and inner peace]. And let endurance have its perfect result and do a thorough work, so that you may be perfect and completely developed [in your faith], lacking in nothing".
Joshua 1:2-4

Eighteen years ago, when God gave me a glimpse of the blueprint and vision for Amazing Rare Rubies, I never would have thought in a million years that it would be where it is today. As the organization has matured, I have come to appreciate why He revealed the blueprint to me in pieces rather than all at once. You see, at that time, I was nowhere near becoming the woman that God created me to be let alone qualified to help other women become who they were meant to be. The first glimpse of this vision was the name, Amazing Rare Rubies; I immediately thought to myself, "why this name and what does it mean"?

He guided me to the next glimpse of this vision

Introduction

which was Proverbs chapter thirty-one; the Virtuous Woman, specifically verse ten which states, "Who can find a virtuous wife? For her worth is far above rubies." The study of this scripture led me to research rubies. I figured if God had stated that they are precious and that a virtuous woman is worth more, there must be something special about them.

In researching this precious gemstone, I found that the process that a ruby goes through to become what we see on display in a retail store is highly symbolic of what we go through on a spiritual level as we evolve in our faith. This process is called the diffusion process which I will breakdown and further explain in a moment, but first, let me share a tidbit of information I learned about the ruby itself. Rubies are valued gemstones dating back centuries; known for their vibrant red color. Rubies consists of crystallized corundum with a small percentage of chromium oxide, which creates varying shades ranging from pinkish red to purple. A common representation is of love and passion, its name comes from the Latin word Ruber, meaning red. The characteristics of a Ruby exemplify strength, quality, and value and are often given in celebration of the birth of a daughter. Rubies are one of the most desirable

Introduction

gemstones because of its hardness, durability, luster, and rarity. And although tough, a Ruby is still subject to chipping and fracture if handled roughly; therefore, care should be taken to ensure it is properly handled. I also learned that natural Rubies have flaws called inclusions; this distinguishes them from imitations that have a tendency to be flawless; this is what makes them unique. It means that the Ruby is not supposed to be flawless but rather it is the inclusions that make them perfectly imperfect. Are you making the symbolic connections here? I was astonished at the revelations God was giving me through the symbolism of a rock and my spiritual growth, but it made so much sense! It was then, I completely understood why He chose the Ruby to set the standard and symbolize the type of woman he intended for us to be. He revealed to me that we are already equipped with every trait, quality and characteristic we will ever need to serve our purpose this lifetime.

Now that you have a basic understanding of the Ruby itself, lets go back and discuss the diffusion process. To keep things in layman's terms, I have summarized this process into seven steps.

In the first step, the Ruby is pre-polished to eradicate any impurities that may affect the diffusion

Introduction

process. Symbolically and spiritually, this is the process where God places you in a state of mind and position which forces you to rid yourself of any persons or situations that may hinder your spiritual journey.

In the second step, the Ruby is cleaned with hydrogen fluoride. This chemical compound has very strong corrosive qualities and the affect it has on the Ruby is to weaken and gradually destroy coarseness. Likewise, God cleanses us through baptism both literally and spiritually with a renewed mind.

In the third step, the Ruby is exposed to a diffusion heat treatment which is considered to be a "natural enhancement," as it is a continuation of the natural process that occurs in the earth when the Ruby was originally formed. During treatment, the Ruby is heated to very high temperatures, almost to its melting point, causing any remaining impurities to reform themselves and change color; this process is permanent and irreversible. As you can probably already tell, this third step is the climax of the diffusion process. Here, God presents the adversities, tribulations and obstacles (testing and pushing us almost to a breaking point)   necessary for renewal, transformation and rebirth---this spiritual rebirth, mimicking the natural birthing process beginning when you were formed in the womb. The fact that this step in the process is irreversible and permanent, it reminds us that our salvation can never be taken from us and that absolutely nothing can ever remove us from the hands of God.

In the fourth step, the Ruby goes through a natural cooling process at perfect temperature as not to alter any of the changes that were made during the diffusion process. This is the calm after the storm and the opportunity to operate as our "new selves" putting into practice and applying the things we learned during our diffusion process. Step four is crucially important because in step five, if the Ruby did not meet the set standards after cooling, it is subject to reprise the diffusion and cooling process; in some cases, 3 to 4 times. Now, I know that may seem tragic but consider this, the Ruby is heated to very high temperatures almost to its melting point.

The same goes for us, God will never put us under more pressure than what He knows we are capable of handling. Furthermore, no two Rubies are the same and they are unique and known for their own individual inclusions and brilliance. Similarly, we all come from different walks of life and have our own unique callings and purpos-

Introduction

es to fulfill which may require varying lengths of time and frequency in the diffusion process; depending on the lessons you are required to learn at that time.

Once you have successfully mastered the diffusion and cooling process for that lesson, you are re-polished in step six. Your crown of glory is awarded to you. You are reminded of who you are and of your divinity as a child of God. He's restoring the years you've sown in tears, so to speak.

And now, in step seven, a protective coating is applied to the Ruby. A seal of protection to cover you and to certify that you are more than qualified to do what God has created you to do here on this Earth. You are equipped and approved by God to uniquely fulfill your purpose and shine your brilliance, becoming the woman He created you to be.........

I want to help you maintain your Ruby brilliance. By practicing your Ruby Traits, you prevent potential resurfacing of any impurities you were eradicated of during your diffusion and cooling process, and Amazing Rare Rubies can help you do just that. The best way to use this devotional and journal is to be engaged with it.

Document and take note of your feelings, learnings and observations of what is working for you and what is not working for you and why. Above all, I urge you to consider prayer in all things and to keep God in every decision made, lesson learned, and message taught.

Page Layout

For each page which introduces a Ruby trait, you will find the following:

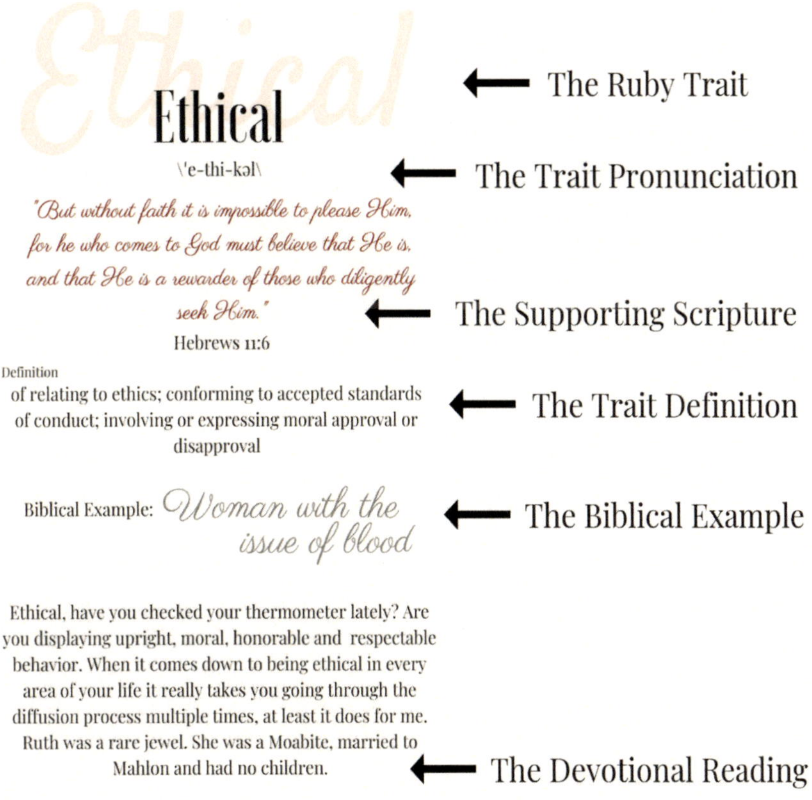
Ethical
Ethical
\'e-thi-kəl\
"But without faith it is impossible to please Him, for he who comes to God must believe that He is, and that He is a rewarder of those who diligently seek Him."
Hebrews 11:6
Definition
of relating to ethics; conforming to accepted standards of conduct; involving or expressing moral approval or disapproval
Biblical Example: Woman with the issue of blood
Ethical, have you checked your thermometer lately? Are you displaying upright, moral, honorable and respectable behavior. When it comes down to being ethical in every area of your life it really takes you going through the diffusion process multiple times, at least it does for me. Ruth was a rare jewel. She was a Moabite, married to Mahlon and had no children.
The Ruby Trait
The Trait Pronunciation
The Supporting Scripture
The Trait Definition
The Biblical Example
The Devotional Reading

The Traits

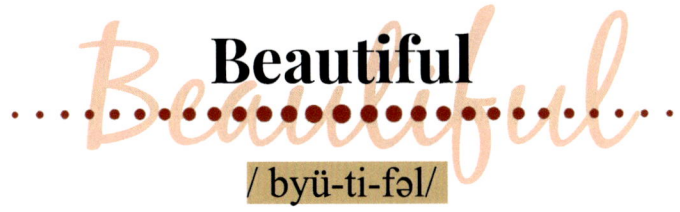

Beautiful

/ byü-ti-fəl/

"rather let it be the hidden person of the heart, with the incorruptible beauty of a gentle and quiet spirit, which is very precious in the sight of God"

1 Peter 3:4

Definition

having qualities of beauty: the quality or aggregate of qualities in a person or thing that gives pleasure to the senses or pleasurably exalts the mind or spirit

Biblical Example: *Rachel*

Beautiful, for she is fearfully and wonderfully made.
A Ruby is unique and captivating. Just like the Ruby gem, a woman is beautiful inside and out. Sometimes we need to work on our inner beauty more than our outer beauty which is part of why we go through the diffusion process. A Ruby is

Beautiful

not conceited nor vain, her beauty shines from the inside out. For she knows that fleshly beauty is fleeting yet she still takes care of her external beauty as well.

She ensures that she keeps herself looking radiant for God, her spouse, her children, family and friends. She carries her beauty with elegance and grace.

Throughout my journey of becoming the woman God created me to be, I have had to go through the diffusion process more than I care to admit when it comes down to my inner beauty versus my outer beauty. I have allowed my flesh and arrogance to promote my external beauty at times and had to eradicate impurities because of it. Remember, "external" beauty is fleeting, but she who fears the Lord, shall be praised.

_____

_____

_____

_____

Beautiful

Beautiful

Comfort

/'kəmfərt/

"Be still, and know that I am God; I will be exalted among the nations, I will be exalted in the earth!"
"Casting all your cares upon Him, for He cares for you."

Psalms 46:10 & 1 Peter 5:7

Definition

> to ease the grief or trouble; to give strength and hope

Biblical Example: *Pharaoh's Daughter*

Comfort, isn't it wonderful and great to know that God sent us a comforter. When we encounter frustration and we need comfort, the word tells us in Psalms 46:10 "be still and know that I am God. I will be exalted among the nations, I will be exalted in the earth!" The word tells us to be still. When we are in need of comfort we need to quiet ourselves be still and prepare to receive the comforter from God.

We are to cast all of our cares on Him because

Comfort

He cares for us. When my husband and I started our first business, frustration seemed to take over every day . But when we took the time, to look at the blessing God was giving us, we begin to take comfort in knowing that none of this would be happening without the hand of God. Remember, God did not leave us alone. As you practice the ruby trait comfort, you as a ruby begin to comfort others remember to be still so that you can receive and give.

Comfort

Comfort

Courage

/ˈkərij/

"Be strong and of good courage, do not fear nor be afraid of them; for the Lord your God, He is the One who goes with you. He will not leave you nor forsake you."

Deuteronomy 31:6

Definition

mental or moral strength to venture, persevere, and withstand danger, fear, or difficulty

Biblical Example: *Esther*

Courage is a very powerful trait. Sometimes the area in your life that you decide to be courageous in will not only be challenging for you but it also could be challenging for people in your life. When I was in over $30,000 worth of debt and I decided that I no longer wanted to be a product of paycheck to paycheck living, I quickly and painfully learned that there would be people in my life that I would have to let go of.

Courage

Not because I didn't love them or care for them but because I was at a place in my life that was foreign to them. When people are accustomed to doing the same thing over and over again it becomes a place of comfort for them and as long as they are surviving they don't see a need to change. Courage requires you to change, broaden your horizons and expand your comfort zone. Stepping outside of my comfort zone financially caused me to take ownership of my contribution to my debt. As you step up to the plate to be courageous in different areas of your life you will find that you need to examine your awareness zone and take responsibility of who you are and where you are.

Courage

Courage

Creative

/krē-ˈā-tiv/

" He has filled them with skill to do all manner of work of the engraver and the designer and the tapestry maker, in blue, purple, and scarlet thread, and fine linen, and of the weaver—those who do every work and those who design artistic works.."

Exodus 35:35

Definition

marked by the ability or power to create; having the quality of something created rather than imitated

Biblical Example: *Widow of Zarephath*

Creative, uniquely, fearfully and wonderfully made. Having this characteristic inside of each and everyone of us support the uniqueness of a ruby becoming. A ruby has inclusions that identifies its uniqueness from other rubies. Our creativity is one of the identifiers that sets us apart from other women.

This is why we have different taste when it

Creative

comes to clothing, food, and much more. Our creativity allows us to create what makes us happy, to create an environment or a life that shows who we are. Are you using your creativity for good, is it bringing joy to you and others in your life?

I challenge you to use your creative juices, to inspire yourself and others. What will you be creative about today?

_____

_____

_____

_____

_____

_____

_____

Creative

Creative

Decision Making

/di-'si-zhən/

"Finally whatever things are noble, whatever things are just, whatever things are pure, whatever things are lovely, whatever things are of good report, if there is any virtue and if there is anything praiseworthy —meditate on these things."

Phillipians 4:8

Definition

to make a final choice or judgment to select as a course of action

Biblical Example: *Deborah*

When we make a decision in our life, it is important that we weigh our options. We must look at the pros and the cons to understand the potential impact of our decisions. I made a decision many years ago that I wanted to have a better relationship, if you have heard my testimony you know that I am a three-time divorcee. I had to realize and accept that in all three of

Decision Making

those divorces, I was the common denominator. So when I decided to be a better person when it came to relationships, I had to address a list of cons that equated to me. As you embark on your journey to make better decisions in your life, ensure that you assess your contributions to the decisions that you have made that have gotten you to where you are today.

_____

_____

_____

_____

_____

_____

_____

_____

_____

Decision Making

Decision Making

Determination

/di-tər-mə-'nā-shən/

" Blessed is the man who endures temptation; for when he has been approved, he will receive the crown of life which the Lord has promised to those who love Him.."

James 1:12

Definition

firm or fixed intention to achieve a desired end

Biblical Example: *Abigail*

Determination. A trait that says " I am going to make it happen". Abagail (Nabal's wife) was determined to reach David to stop him from killing her family due to her husbands foolish behavior. She convinced David that he was a better man and to allow God to take vengeance upon her husband.

When we really want something in life we have determination inside of use to make it happen. How determined are you to become the woman

Determination

you were created to be?
As for me, I will become EVERYTHING that He created me to be. Join me!
Speak it, Own it, Claim whose you are and start your journey to becoming.

Determination

Determination

Diligent

/ˈdi-lə-jənt/

"The soul of a lazy man desires, and has nothing; But the soul of the diligent shall be made rich."

Proverbs 13:4

Definition

characterized by steady, earnest, and energetic effort

Biblical Example: *Hannah*

Diligently seek self. Are you doing something thoroughly and well for yourself? Being diligent is a skill that every Ruby needs. Being Diligent means that you are able to focus and concentrate to complete any task at hand. Being diligent requires self-discipline so that you can accomplish your goals, whether they are personal goals, professional goals or spiritual goals. Being diligent means you're willing to learn and with practice you will become an expert in what-

Diligent

ever you're diligently seeking.
Remember someone once said "you can have a good day tomorrow, if you start today".
Start becoming today.

Diligent

Diligent

Ethical

/'e-thi-kəl/

"But without faith it is impossible to please Him, for he who comes to God must believe that He is, and that He is a rewarder of those who diligently seek Him."

Hebrews 11:6

Definition

of relating to ethics; conforming to accepted standards of conduct; involving or expressing moral approval or disapproval

Biblical Example: *Woman with the issue of blood*

Ethical, have you checked your thermometer lately? Are you displaying upright, moral, honorable and respectable behavior. When it comes down to being ethical in every area of your life it really takes you going through the diffusion process multiple times, at least it does for me. Ruth was a rare jewel. She was a Moabite, married to

Mahlon and had no children. When her husband was killed in Moab and she was left alone, I could only imagine that in her mind she wanted to do some pretty unethical things because it seemed like life was not being kind to her. However Ruth took the highroad by staying with her mother-in-law Naomi and returning to Judah with her. Ruth showed us that God hears and responds to His peoples cry. Although it is not easy to do the right thing all the time, I have learned that when we do the right thing, God will do greater things. So when the opportunity presents it self to you and you have a choice to do an ethical act or an unethical act, I challenge you to do the ethical act. Remember every action causes a reaction. Check your ethical thermometer. Let's do this!!

_____

_____

_____

_____

Ethical

Ethical

Faith

/'fāth/

"But without faith it is impossible to please Him, for he who comes to God must believe that He is, and that He is a rewarder of those who diligently seek Him."

Hebrews 11:6

Definition

firm belief in something for which there is no proof; something that is believed especially with strong conviction

Biblical Example: *Woman with the issue of blood*

Faith, without it we cannot please God. Faith requires us to believe in something bigger, better and higher than ourselves. This trait is one that causes me to check my "Awareness Zone" of who I am and where I am when dealing with difficult situations. Although we only need faith the size of a mustard seed it can be hard sometimes to even have that mustard seed size faith. When I find myself struggling with my faith, I remember that I cannot please God if I don't stand on His word and the power He has to move mountains for me, with me and through me. Being a three-time divorcee, I did have doubt that I could ever find and have a solid happy marriage. Honing in on that mustard seed of faith and wanting a better relationship for myself, I begin to work on myself, to better myself and I found that with my little effort God could and would do big things. Stand on your mustard seed of faith and watch God work miracles in your life.

Faith

Faith

Focus

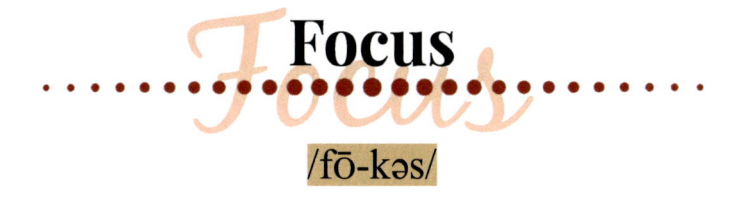

/fō-kəs/

"Set your mind on things above, not on things on the earth."

Colossians 3:2

Definition

a center of activity, attraction, or attention; a state or condition permitting clear perception or understanding

Biblical Example: *Mary of Bethany*

Focus, a Ruby knows that you get what you work for; not what you wish for. Jumping from one thing to another starts a cycle of not completing things. A ruby knows not to allow people to destroy her hopes and dreams with their words and actions. She knows that she cannot be inconsistent in her life and expect to accomplish her dreams and desires. She continuously

Focus

looks at how she can press forward.

When I was a single mom of two, I went through a period of losing focus on life and it impacted not only me but my children also. My lack of focus caused me to be in debt, unhappy at a job, and unable to hold down and keep a solid relationship. I jump from one relationship to the next not understanding that my actions were taking me off point when it came to my life goals and purpose.

Stay focused and remember you get what you work for.

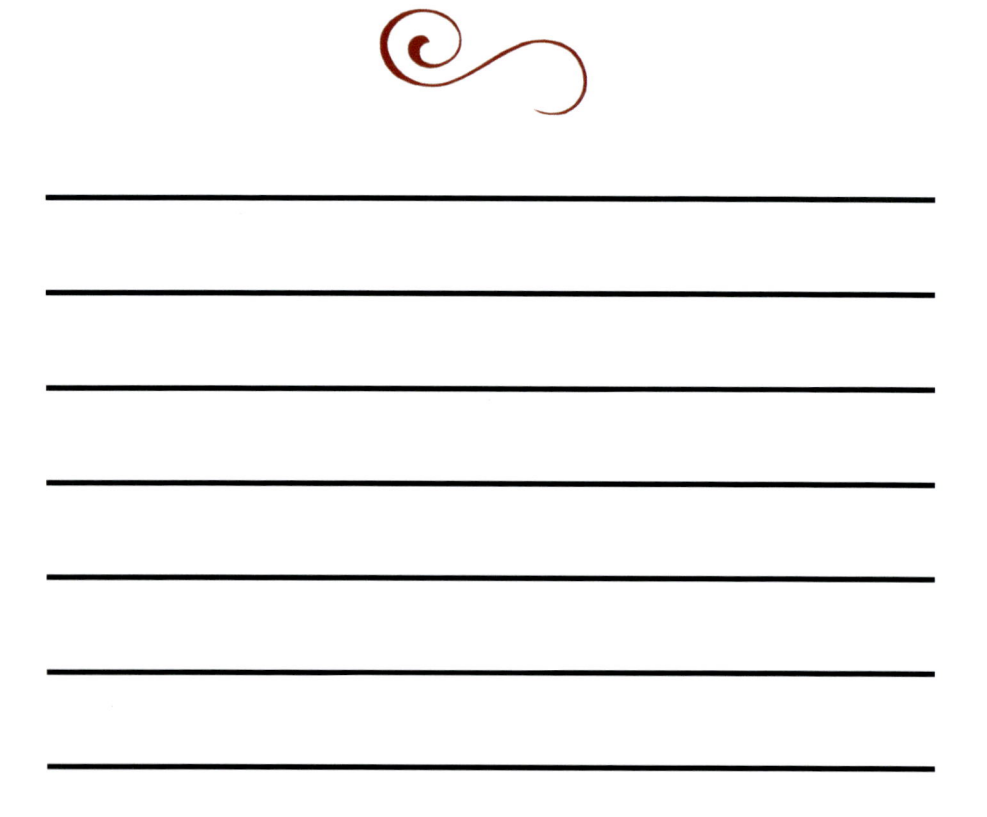

_____

_____

_____

_____

_____

_____

Focus

Forgiveness

/fər-ˈgiv-nəs/

"Take heed to yourselves. If your brother sins against you, rebuke him; and if he repents, forgive him. And if he sins against you seven times in a day, and seven times in a day returns to you, saying, 'I repent,' you shall forgive him.".

Luke 17:3-4

Definition

to cease to feel resentment against (an offender)

Biblical Example: *Ruth*

Forgiveness is one of the traits that appears to play a big role in every Ruby becoming the woman she was created to be. Letting go of anger, hurt, resentment and frustration requires us to realize and accept that the situation which caused all of those symptoms is over. Until we come to that realization, we cannot move for-

Forgiveness

ward. In my 50 plus years of life I had to learned how to forgive and let go of people, things, emotions, hurts, thoughts and curses.

Failing to forgive is a curse and being unforgiving will block your blessings.

Make a decision to forgive and let go of the past. Stop playing the victim card and blaming others. When you forgive yourself and forgive others, you will set yourself free mentally, emotionally, spiritually, and physically.

Forgiveness

Forgiveness

Giving

/'gi-veeg/

"So let each one give as he purposes in his heart, not grudgingly or of necessity; for God loves a cheerful giver.."

2 Corinthians 9:7

Definition

freely devote, set aside, or sacrifice for a purpose;bestow (love, affection, or other emotional support)

Biblical Example: *Tabitha a.k.a Dorcas*

Giving, Jesus said it best in John 6:35 "I am the bread that gives life. If you come to My table and eat, you will never go hungry. Believe in Me, and you will never go thirsty." A Ruby is giving, she extends her hand to the poor she helps those in need, she supports and gives to her family and friends. She provides food, clothing,

Giving

godly wisdom and spiritual support. She provides hope in a dark and dismal world. She gives from her heart, her mind, her emotions and her spirit. Giving is one of the traits that Amazing Rare Rubies rests in, because we are all about giving that beacon of hope that helps women to become. Be a support system that gives another woman Hope. Start today!!!

Giving

Giving

Humble

/həm-bəl/

"But without faith it is impossible to please Him, for he who comes to God must believe that He is, and that He is a rewarder of those who diligently seek Him."

Hebrews 11:6

Definition

not proud or haughty: not arrogant or assertive; reflecting, expressing, or offered in a spirit of deference or submission

Biblical Example: *Woman with the issue of blood*

Humble yourself, for the first shall be last and the last shall be first. Take Mary, the mother of Jesus, she is one of the humblest women in the Bible, in my opinion.
A virgin who God chose to birth Jesus. Can you imagine the head rolling, the finger-pointing, backstabbing and social media scrutiny she ex-

perienced?

But Mary response to God was "I am a servant of the Lord; let it be to me according to your word "Luke 1:38. Are you a servant of the Lord? Are you being obedient and walking out your process to becoming the woman you were created to be? Are you triumphant over the trials and tribulations of your diffusion process?

We should all be saying "bring on the heat" because we are ready to become. Come on, walk with me through this diffusion process. We can cool down naturally together.

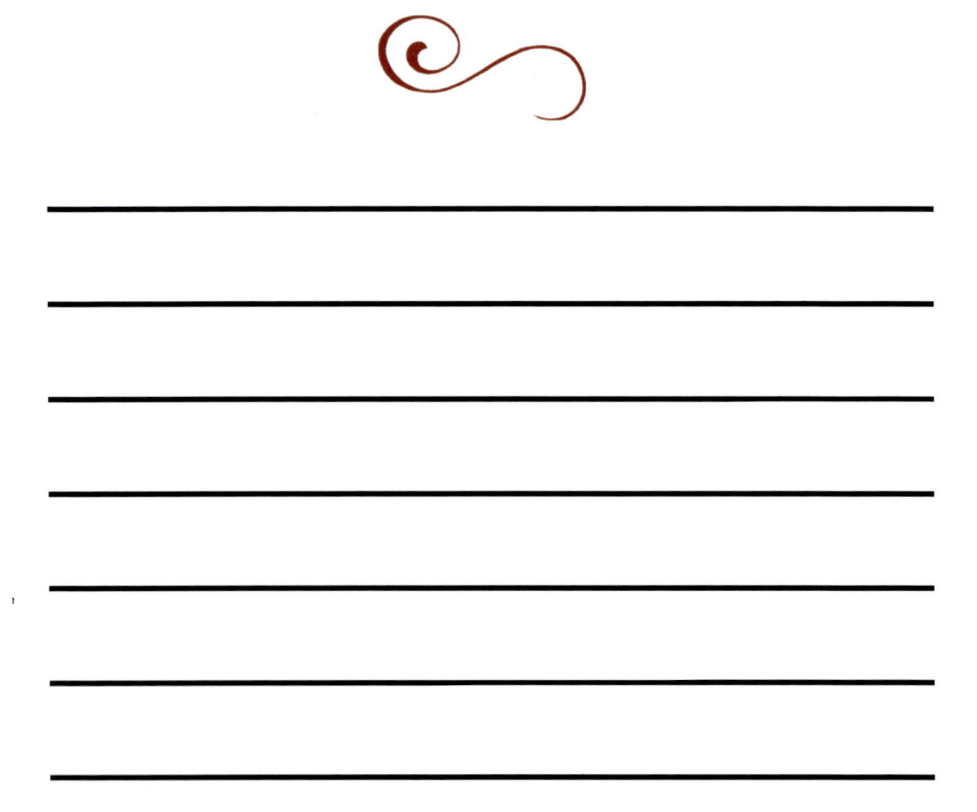

_____

_____

_____

_____

_____

_____

_____

Humble

Humble

Loving

/ləving/

"Love suffers long and is kind; love does not envy; love does not parade itself, is not puffed up; does not behave rudely, does not seek its own, is not provoked, thinks no evil; does not rejoice in iniquity, but rejoices in the truth; bears all things, believes all things, hopes all things, endures all things"

1 Corinthians 13:4-7

Definition

feeling or showing love or great care; warmly affectionate

Biblical Example: *Ruth*

Loving you is easy because you are beautiful. If only that were true, right? To love someone requires us to accept them as is, their flaws and all. In one of my favorite movies, there is a scene between two male characters and one asks the other, how did you know that your wife truly loves

Loving

you? And the other male responds, "because she knows everything about me and she is still here".

How powerful is that! That, my friend, is unconditional love. That is how God loves us, He knows everything about us and He is still with us.

Who are you loving unconditionally? Whose feelings, heart and emotions are you putting above yours? Do you have a Corinthian's love with your spouse? You know that Eros and Agape love? Do you have a Philia and Storge brotherly love for your friends and family?

I dare you to love unconditionally. I dare you to be a loving Ruby. Do you accept my challenge?

_____

_____

_____

_____

_____

Loving

Loving

Obedience

/ō-'bē-dē-ən(t)sə/

"If you fully obey the Lord your God and carefully follow all his commands I give you today, the Lord your God will set you high above all the nations on earth."

Deuteronomy 28:1

Definition

to follow the commands or guidance of; an act or instance of obeying;

Biblical Example: *Sarah*

Obedience is better than sacrifice. We have all heard that one before. To be obedient to God's word is better than anything that we can offer sacrificially.
A Ruby can become who God has called her to be when she realizes that being obedient to God will automatically bring joy, peace and happiness to her life.
When we are obedient to "whose" we are we cannot fail.

Obedience

When I decided to begin my journey to becoming the woman God created me to be, I then became obedient to HOW my purpose was supposed to be carried out.

This is when Amazing Rare Rubies was conceived. Although, I still don't see everything round how God wants me to do this, I know that because I am being obedient to what He has called me to do, my works are pleasing in His sight. Will you align your behavior to be obedient to becoming the woman you were created to be?

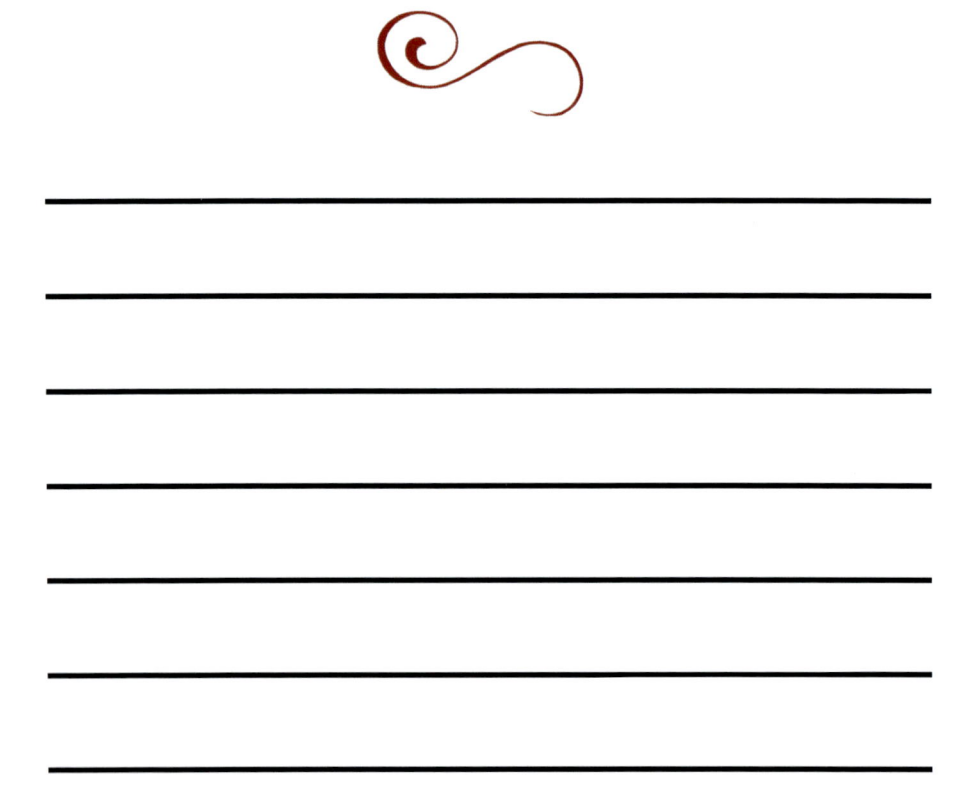

_____

_____

_____

_____

_____

_____

Obedience

Obedience

Patience

/'pāSHəns/

"But if we hope for what we do not yet have, we wait for it patiently"

Romans 8:25

Definition

the capacity to accept or tolerate delay, trouble, or suffering without getting angry or upset

Biblical Example: *Elizabeth*

Patience, now here is a trait that requires self control and restraint. James 5:7-8 says "be patient therefore brothers until the coming of the Lord. See how the farmer waits for the precious fruit of the earth, being patient about it, until he receives the early in the late rains. You also be patient.
Establish your hearts for the coming of the Lord is at hand".

Patience

I love movies and in one that I watch pretty often there is a scene where one man tells another man a story. He said, There were two farmers who desperately needed rain, they both prayed for the rain but only one worked his field. When the rain came which one do you think receive the blessing?

This story challenges us to wait on the Lord. The rain may not come when you want it too but it is always on time. Be like Elizabeth, John the Baptist mother, be patient for the blessing is coming.

Patience

Patience

Prepared
/'pri-'perd/

"She is not afraid of snow for her household, For all her household is clothed with scarlet

Proverbs 31:21

Definition

to have made (something) ready for use or consideration

Biblical Example: *The Virtuous Woman*

Prepared, come what may. The difference between being reactive and proactive is preparation. Planning is organized success while Preparation is actionable success. Are you prepared for the harvest when God sends it? Are you praying and working?

I love the proverbs 31 woman because in verse 21, it says "she is not afraid of snow for her household, for all of her household is close with Scarlet". That tells me that she is prepared for the winter storm. She is prepared for the unexpected. She has already taken care of her household and insured they are clothed in Scarlet.

Are you ready to become? Are you prepared for the abundant life of being the woman God created you to be?

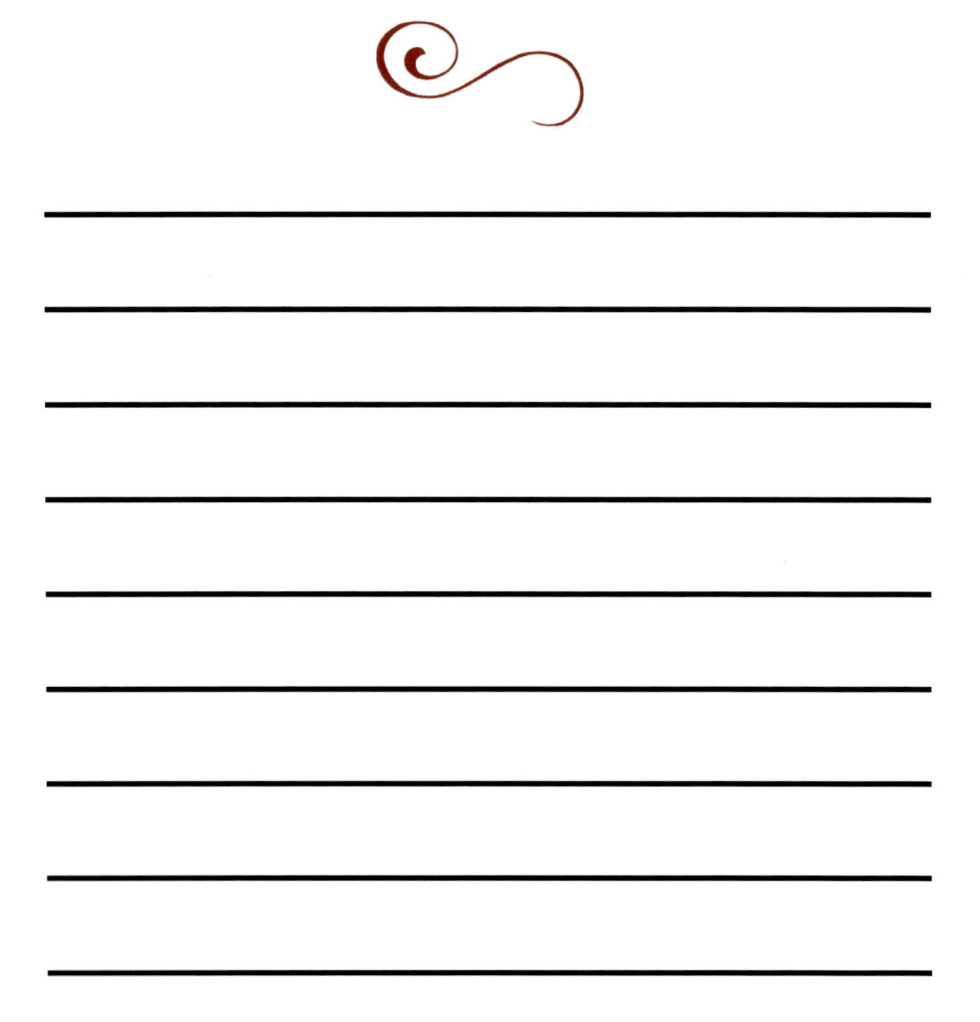

_____

_____

_____

_____

_____

_____

_____

_____

Prepared

Prepared

Selfless

/'selfləs/

"But Hannah did not go up, for she said to her husband, "Not until the child is weaned; then I will take him, that he may appear before the Lord and remain there forever"

1 Samuel 1:2-21

Definition

concerned more with the needs and wishes of others than with one's own; unselfish

Biblical Example: *Hannah*

Selfless is a very challenging trait. Because it requires us to step into territory that seems foreign to the world we live in today. Being selfless challenges us to openly show that we are willing to put others before we put ourselves. As a married woman, I have had to learn a thing or two about being selfless.

It is not always easy to put another flawed human being above yourself. Learning to respect God's hierarchy in marriage (God first, then the husband, then the wife, and then the children) has helped me to hone my selfless trait. To give to a person without expectation of something in return has opened my mind and my heart to unconditional love and I must tell you, God has blessed me abundantly for my selfless acts. I challenge you to do one selfless act per day for the next seven days and expect nothing in return.

Selfless

Selfless

Thrifty

/'thrif-tē/

"All these people gave their gifts out of their wealth; but she out of her poverty put in all she had to live on"

Luke 21:1-4

Definition

(of a person or their behavior) using money and other resources carefully and not wastefully

Biblical Example: *The Widowed Woman*

Thrifty, now this trait is like a command from Jesus. John 6:12 tells us that after everyone was full, Jesus said to His disciples "gather up the leftover fragments so that nothing will be lost". Proverbs 31:27 says "she looks well to the ways of her household and does not eat the bread of idleness".

Thrifty

We should not waste what God has entrusted us with.

To come from a lifestyle of living paycheck to paycheck to a lifestyle of abundant living, I had to learn and practice the importance of being thrifty.

I had to learn how to be a good steward over the things God had given me. One thing I learned was how to budget my money down to zero to make sure I knew where every penny went. I developed a mindset to tell my money where I wanted it to go versus my money going where it wanted to go. You honor God when you honor what he has given you,

I encourage you to also honor yourself with what you have worked for, be thrifty with the resources you have, use them wisely not wastefully. I challenge you start measuring where your resources are going today.

_____

_____

_____

Thrifty

Thrifty

Stable Minded

/stābəl/

"Therefore take up the whole armor of God, that you may be able to withstand in the evil day, and having done all, to stand. Stand therefore, having girded your waist with truth, having put on the breastplate of righteousness"

Ephesians 6:13-14

Definition

(of a person) sane and sensible; not easily upset or disturbed; not likely to change or fail; firmly established

Biblical Example: *Puah & Shiphrah*

Stable minded, she is standing firm on who she was created to be, her mind is stable, her spirit is stable, her life is stable. She is not double minded, she is not going to and fro, she is standing firm on who she is. She doesn't give up her ground.

She has drawn a line in the sand and she will not allow anyone to trample on her expectations, her wellness, her spirituality, her marriage, her finances or any ground that belongs to her. A stable minded Ruby knows that we are a chosen people and that we belong to God. It is time to take your ground back and to stand firm because strength and honor are your clothing. When I was struggling with my finances, and I was going to and fro on saving money and not saving money, I found myself in very lukewarm territory that provided no stability. I had to pick a side and decide if I wanted to be stable or unstable. Which one are you?

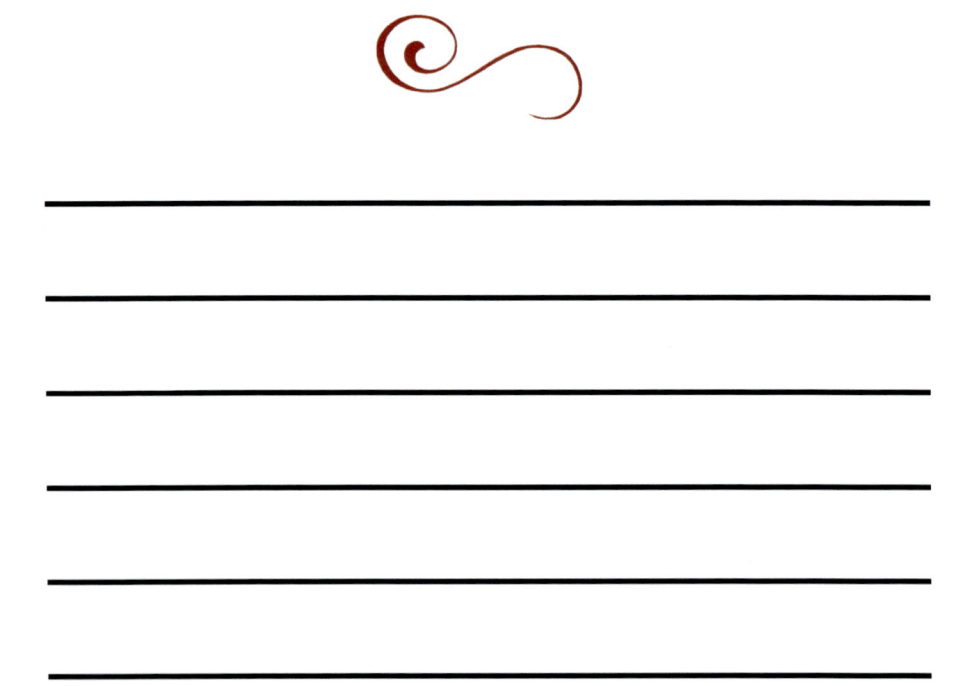

Stable Minded

Stable Minded

Strong

/'strōNG/

"Because the Lord has heard that I am unloved, He has therefore given me this son also"

Genesis Chapters 29&30

Definition

(of a person's character) showing determination, self- control, and good judgment; able to withstand great force or pressure

Biblical Example: *Leah*

Strong and courageous they both go hand-in-hand.
Joshua 1:6 says "be strong and of good courage" 1Chronicles 28:20 says "be strong and courageous" 2Chronicles 32:7 says "be strong and courageous" Joshua 10:25 says "be strong and courageous".
Did you get the point here? God repeatedly tells

Strong

us to be strong and courageous. Then we see the proverbs 31 woman being strong and courageous. Wow. Be strong ladies, weakness won't last always if you are diligently seeking to become.

Strong

Strong

Thoughtful

/'thȯt-fəl/

"There is a time for everything, and a season for every activity under the heavens"

Ecclesiastes 3:1

Definition

showing consideration for the needs of other people; showing careful consideration or attention

Biblical Example: *The Shunammite Woman*

Thoughtful is more than a mental (thinking) trait. Being thoughtful requires you to show consideration for others.
So being thoughtful is an action word. You can display thoughtful acts through actions like remembering to tell a person happy birthday or showing support in their time of need.

Thoughtful

Being thoughtful of others is a selfless act. When I was a single mom, caring for and showing acts of thoughtfulness was part of life with my children. If you are a mother, I am sure you can relate. It is your motherly instinct to take care of your children. Now in other areas we may need to focus more on these acts like at work or with our spouse or friends. Place positive thoughts in your mind that support positive actions.

Thoughtful

Thoughtful

Timely

/ˈtīm-lē/

"There is a time for everything, and a season for every activity under the heavens"

Ecclesiastes 3:1

Definition

coming early or at the right time; appropriate or adapted to the times or the occasion

Biblical Example: *Esther*

Timely is a trait that encompasses a word that we can never get back once it is gone and that word is TIME. How you spend your time, being on time, and doing things timely is all part of being a Ruby. A Ruby understands the importance of being on time, finishing her task in a timely manner and when she should start a task.

Practicing the ruby trait timely challenges us to

Timely

be a woman of our word and to do what we say we're going to do. I personally keep an organizer, in addition to my iPhone LOL, to help me stay on track regarding my schedule for my personal life and my business life. We all have a lot of things to juggle and it's important that we do each of them. Start managing your time today.

Timely

Timely

Trustworthy

/ˈtrəs(t)wərTHē/

"A gossip betrays a confidence, but a trustworthy person keeps a secret"

Proverbs 11:13

Definition

worthy of confidence; able to be relied on as honest or truthful

Biblical Example: *Mary Mother of Jesus*

Trustworthy, yes she is. A Ruby is a confidant to a person in need. A person can rest in knowing that a Ruby will not double cross them. Proverbs 31:11 says "he safely trust his heart with her". Your heart is the one organ you cannot live without. For a husband to safely trust his heart with his wife, she definitely has to be a woman of noble character and who's worth is far above

Rubies.

Consider Mary, Mother of Jesus, who was trusted to birth and raise the Christ, God's only begotten son. Wow! So ask yourself, are you developing a trustworthy character? Ask yourself do the people in your life, safely trust their heart with you, their concerns, their hopes, and their dreams?

_____

_____

_____

_____

_____

_____

_____

_____

Trustworthy

Trustworthy

Wisdom

/ˈwizdəm/

"Get wisdom, get understanding; do not forget my words or turn away from them. Do not forsake wisdom, and she will protect you; love her, and she will watch over you."

Proverbs 4:5-6

Definition

the quality of having experience, knowledge, and good judgment; the quality of being wise

Biblical Example: *Queen Sheba*

Wisdom, don't you just love Proverbs 31:26, she opens her mouth with wisdom. This means she uses good judgement. I believe she knew Ecclesiastes "a time to speak" Lol. Queen of Sheba, Makeda, used wisdom when she decided to seek a partnership with King Solomon after seeing and witnessing his abundant kingdom and wisdom.

Wisdom

Because she had seen this with her own eyes, she was certain that God would continue to use Solomon for the success of Israel.

I encourage you to seek wisdom for yourself. Take opportunities to expand your knowledge base.

Learn from others who are growing where you are going. What would you challenge yourself to seek wisdom about today?

_____

_____

_____

_____

_____

_____

_____

_____

Wisdom

Wisdom

Made in the USA
Columbia, SC
22 December 2018